Factfile Cymru
Animals in Wales

interesting

strange

amazing

unbelievable

excellent

cool

This Pont book was first published in Welsh in 2013 by
Gomer Press, Llandysul, Ceredigion, SA44 4JL
under the title *A Wyddoch Chi am Anifeiliaid Cymru.*
ISBN 978 1 84851 741 7
A CIP record for this title is available from the British Library.
© Copyright text: Elin Meek, 2013
© Copyright illustrations: Eric Heyman, 2013
Elin Meek and Eric Heyman have asserted their moral right under the
Copyright, Designs and Patents Act, 1988
to be identified respectively as author and illustrator of this work.
All rights reserved. No part of this book may be reproduced,
stored in a retrieval system, or transmitted in any form
or by any means, electronic, electrostatic, magnetic tape, mechanical,
photocopying, recording or otherwise without permission
in writing from the above publishers.
This book is published with the financial support of the
Welsh Books Council.
Printed and bound in Wales at
Gomer Press, Llandysul, Ceredigion

The publishers would like to thank the following for giving permission to reproduce images in this publication:
Front cover: Shutterstock
Alamy: p. 9 (Mar Photographics), 15 (Corbis Bridge; Paul Doyle), 16 (Andrew Linscott).
Anne Jones: p. 10, 24.
Ingrid Delaitre: p. 13.
PhotolibraryWales.com: p. 7 (David Woodfall), 8 (Pierino Algieri), 12 (Peter Lane), 20 (David Williams).
Shutterstock: p. 6, 7, 8, 9, 10, 11, 12, 13, 14, 15, 16, 17, 18, 19, 20, 21, 22, 23, 24, 25, 26, 27, 28, 29, 30, 31, 32.

Factfile Cymru
Animals in Wales

Elin Meek
Cartoons by **Eric Heyman**

Pont

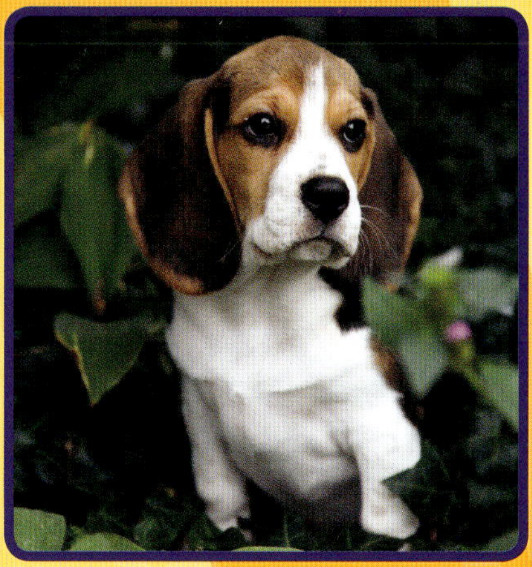
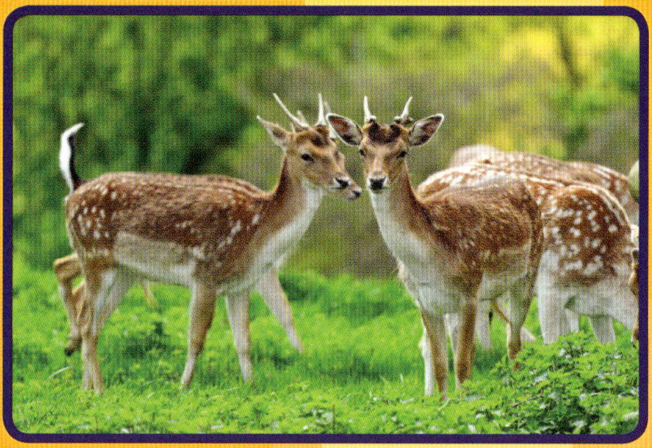
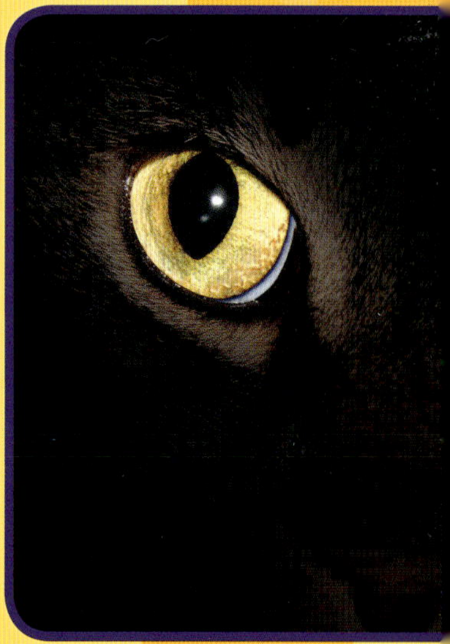
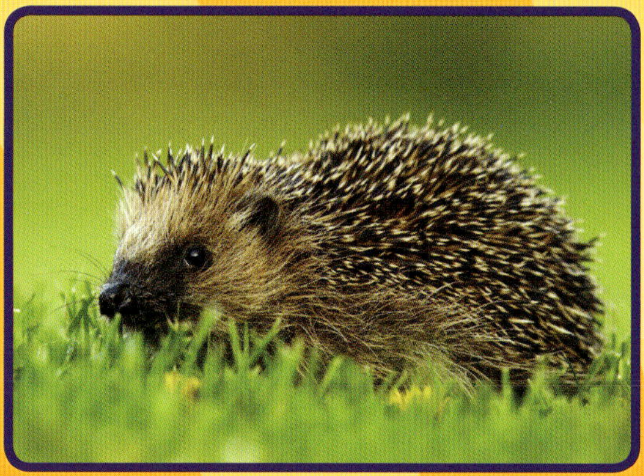
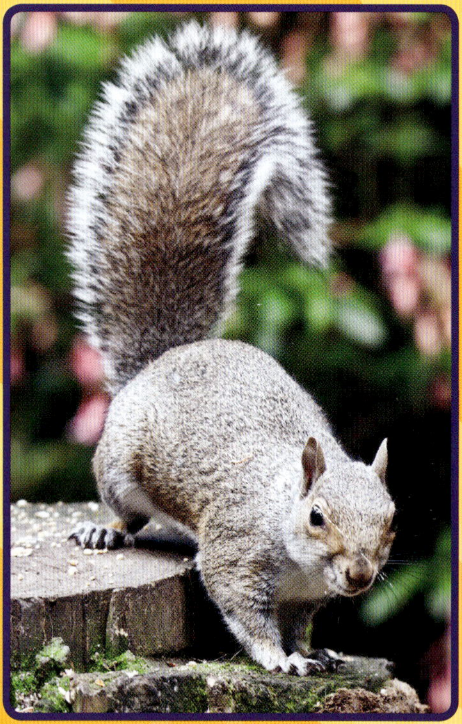
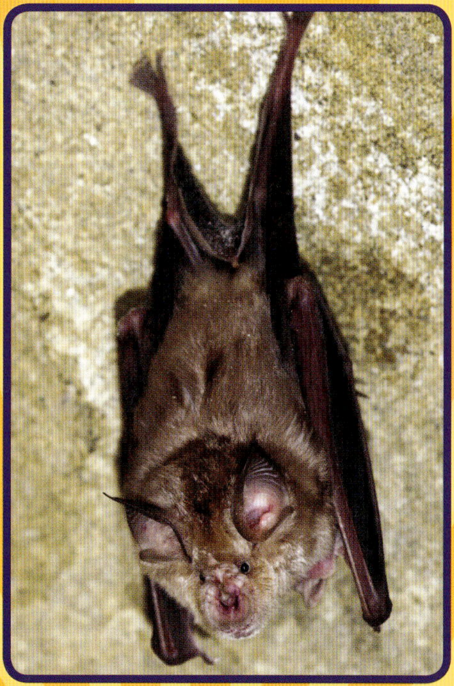

Contents

Farm Animals:
- Cows — 6–7
- Sheep — 8–9
- Pigs — 10–11
- Horses — 12–14

Pets:
- Dogs — 15–17
- Cats — 18–19

Land Mammals:
- Goats — 20–21
- Deer — 22
- Rabbits — 23
- Badgers — 24–25
- Squirrels — 26–27
- Foxes — 28
- Hedgehogs — 29
- Rats — 30–31
- Bats — 32

Index — inside back cover

Farm Animals
Cows

Did you know ...

★ The Celts brought the first cattle to Wales in the Stone Age, around 6,000 years ago.

Q&A

Question: How many cattle are there in Wales today?
Answer: About 500,000 (half a million).

★ Cattle are very valuable because they can produce:
- meat
- milk – which can be turned into cream, butter, cheese, yoghurt and ice cream
- leather (from the animal's skin)
- glue (from its bones and hooves)

Pollution

★ The bacteria in a cow's stomach produce 100 to 200 litres of methane gas every day – as much as a car.

★ If a cow eats garlic it produces less methane.

★ But then the milk has a garlic flavour! *Ych a fi!*

Fact!
A cow's tongue measures 30 centimetres!

Vocabulary

produce: make
bacteria: tiny living organisms
methane: a greenhouse gas damaging to the environment

Did you know ...

Dairy cattle

Q&A

Question: How much milk can a cow produce each day?
Answer: Around 50 litres.

- There are over 250,000 (quarter of a million) dairy cattle in Wales.
- Most of them are Friesians.
- In the summer, a dairy cow eats around 70 kilograms of grass each day!
- The cow uses half the grass just to stay alive and the other half to produce milk.
- Cattle produce more milk after listening to classical music.
- British farmers produce enough milk each year to fill 4,500 Olympic-sized pools!

- **Welsh Black Cattle** are special to Wales.
- They are black and hairy and their horns turn upwards.
- They can cope with Welsh weather – usually cold and wet!
- They are bred for their meat.

Moooooo-re about cattle!

- If you see cattle lying down, it's a sign that it's going to rain.
- Believe it or not, but cattle from different areas are supposed to have a local accent when they moo!
- A cow:
  - can smell something even if it's six miles away
  - likes to lie down for between 12 and 14 hours a day
  - farts (but no one's sure how often!)

Sheep
Did you know ...

- There are over 8,000,000 (yes, eight million) sheep in Wales!
- They outnumber all other animals in Wales.
- In fact there are more Welsh sheep than people!

Q&A
Question: How many breeds of sheep are there in Britain?
Answer: Over 40.

- A group of sheep is called a flock or herd.
- The herd is looked after by a shepherd.
- Sheepdogs are really important to the shepherd's work.

- **Welsh Mountain Sheep** are special to Wales.
- They're the smallest sheep in Britain, but the toughest.
- They can live on the poorest mountain land in the wind and snow.
- Their lambs are born when there's still snow on the ground!

Poor old sheep!
- They can get bad feet after grazing on wet land.
- Because lots of vermin, like maggots, flies and lice, attack their skin, sheep have to be dipped in sheep dip.

Fact!
A lamb knows its own mum by the sound of her bleating.

Vocabulary
vermin: small animals and insects which are harmful to crops, animals or people
sheep dip: a chemical bath which kills off vermin

Did you know …

- Sheep are bred for their meat and their wool.
- Enough meat is produced in Britain every year to make over 250,000,000 (250 million) Sunday dinners.

Shearing

Q&A

Question: How many sheep are shorn in the annual shearing competition at the Royal Welsh Show?
Answer: As many as 5,000.

- Sheep have to be shorn to remove their wool.
- During the summer months some shearers travel from farm to farm.
- There's not a huge amount of wool on the Welsh Mountain Sheep – the fleece usually weighs about 1.5 kilograms.

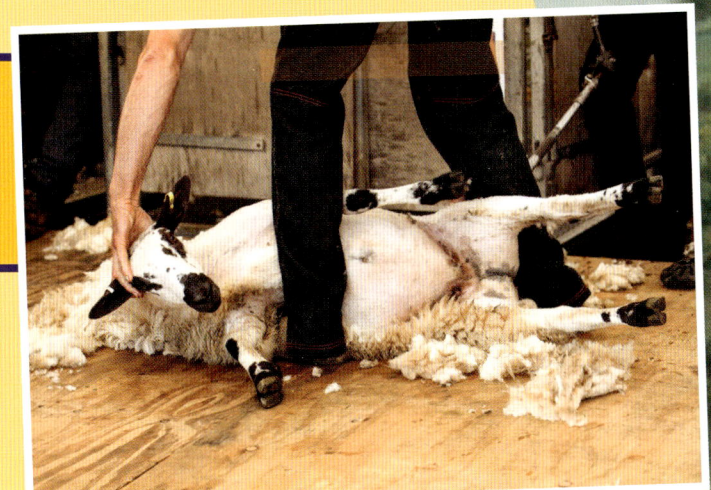

Fact!
The fastest time for shearing a sheep is 45.51 seconds – and the record is held by Dwayne Black from Australia.

- The cattle grid challenge! Some Welsh sheep are experts in getting across cattle grids. They do this by running from a distance, curling themselves into a ball and rolling over the grid to reach the other side!

- Meirion Owen, the champion sheep drover from Carmarthenshire, is also skilled at herding ducks. His sheepdog drives them forward through a tunnel and down a slope.

Vocabulary

shearing: cutting or shaving the fleece from a sheep
fleece: the sheep's woolly coat

Pigs
Did you know ...

- There are around 20,000 pigs in Wales.
- There are two types of pig:
  - pigs bred for their pork
  - pigs bred for bacon

Q&A

Question: What kind of pig is bred in Wales?
Answer: The Welsh pig is bred for its bacon. It's white with ears which turn downwards.

- Pigs grow quickly and they're ready to be sent to the butcher when they are about six to seven months old.

Dirty Pigs

- The pig is not a dirty animal in spite of its 'piggy' reputation.
- Pigs sit in the mud in order to keep cool: unlike us, they can't sweat.
- Mud protects the pig's skin from sunburn and insect bites.
- Hopefully nobody says that your bedroom looks like a 'pigsty'!

Piggy Tricks

- Pigs are intelligent animals and can perform tricks.
- Pigs:
  - use more than 20 different sounds to communicate with each other
  - have a very good sense of smell – if you hide their favourite food in the soil, it's not very long before they find it
  - can run a mile in seven minutes

Fact!

A contented pig rests for more than 82% of its time.

Did you know ...

The olden days
★ Pigs used to be kept in pigsties made of brick or stone. These days they're kept in arks or large sheds.

★ Years ago:
- every farm or cottage kept a pig
- in the slate areas of north Wales and the industrial areas of the south there would be a pig at the bottom of the garden.

★ A family would keep two pigs:
- one to eat
- one to sell in order to pay the rent

Pig-killing day
★ This was a big day, and everyone would share the meat with friends and relations (who would share out their own pig when the time came).

★ The pig's meat would be treated with salt and hung from beams in the house.

Fact!
Pigs have got 44 teeth - people only have 32!

Vocabulary
arks: wooden or metal shelters designed for animals
beams: large timbers which support the roof or ceiling

Horses
Did you know ...

Fact!
There was a horse-like animal in existence 50,000,000 (50 million) years ago.

★ There are two kinds of horse:
- light horses, like the Arab and the Thoroughbred
- heavy horses, like draught horses

★ Years ago, horses used to do lots of heavy work:
- carrying knights wearing heavy armour into battle
- working on arable farms, ploughing or pulling heavy loads
- pulling road vehicles, such as stagecoaches
- pulling narrow boats on the canals
- working in the coal mines

★ These days machines are used instead of horses, but sometimes horses are still used:
- to pull loads of timber in woodland areas
- by the police when patrolling football matches

★ Horses are important to many people's leisure activities. People like to:
- go riding
- take part in horse races
- participate in show-jumping competitions

Vocabulary
draught horses: horses which pull or *draw* heavy loads
arable: land ploughed to grow crops

Q&A
Question: How long does a horse live?
Answer: Between 15 and 20 years.

12

Did you know ...

Q&A
Question: How long is a mare pregnant before her foal is born?
Answer: 11 months.

Foal
★ Foals are able to get up and walk a couple of minutes after they are born. On average it takes about a year for a human baby to walk!
★ Foals are fully grown when they're between three and four years old.

Q&A
Question: How do you measure a horse's height?
Answer: In hands.
★ You have to measure from the floor to the top of the horse's shoulder.
★ Horses are over 14.2 hands in height.
★ A draught horse measures 17 to 20 hands.

Pony
★ Ponies are smaller than horses – under 14.3 hands.
★ They've got strong legs.
★ Welsh ponies and cobs are breeds which are special to Wales.
★ They have their very own organisation: the Welsh Pony and Cob Society.

Carneddau Ponies
★ There have been ponies on the Carneddau Mountains, in Snowdonia, since 500 years before the birth of Christ.
★ These days there are only about 200 of them left.
★ People used to think they were too wild to be ridden, but horse-whisperer Barry Thomas from Crymych has managed to train them.

Vocabulary
hands: the width of a hand, the measurement used for horses

Fact!
Horses don't usually like the smell of pigs!

Did you know ...

* You can tell a horse's age by looking at its teeth.

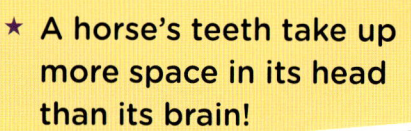

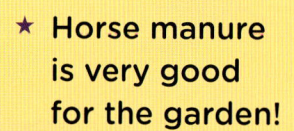

* A horse's teeth take up more space in its head than its brain!

* Horse manure is very good for the garden!

* Horses can't vomit.

* Don't stand behind a horse, in case you get kicked!

* Every horse and pony in Wales has to have its own passport.

Horses on the train!
* In 2011 a man in Wrexham tried to take a horse on the train. He wanted to buy two tickets – one for himself and the other for the horse!
* Later that day, the man tried to take his horse to hospital for medical treatment. But (surprise, surprise) he wasn't allowed to stay!

Madonna's Welsh Cob
* Madonna, the pop star, owns a horse which comes originally from the Tregaron area.

Q&A
Question: What is horsehair?
Answer: The hair from a horse's tail.

14

Pets
Dogs
Did you know ...

★ Dogs come in all shapes and sizes. World-wide there are more than 200 breeds of dog. They include:
  - Beagles
  - West Highland Terriers
  - Cavalier King Charles Spaniels
  - Dalmatians

Beagle

West Highland Terrier

Cavalier King Charles Spaniel

Dalmatian

★ Some dogs are working animals:
  - police dogs
  - sheepdogs
  - hunting dogs
  - gundogs (used by people who shoot game birds like pheasant and grouse)
  - guide dogs for the blind

★ But these days most dogs are kept as pets.

Fact!
Dogs can get sunburn!

★ A dog's sense of smell:
  - is four times better than a cat's
  - and 14 times better than a human's!

★ That's why dogs are used to sniff out drugs at airports.

Did you know ...

Welsh Sheepdogs
- ★ They are unique to Wales.
- ★ They're bigger than other sheepdogs, such as the Border Collie.
- ★ They are often red and white in colour.

Welsh Terriers
- ★ Terriers were originally bred to chase animals, like rats and badgers, which live underground.
- ★ They weigh between nine and ten kilograms.
- ★ They have rectangular-shaped faces.
- ★ They are black and white in colour.

Welsh Corgis
- ★ There are two types of corgi – the Pembroke and the Cardigan corgi.
- ★ The word 'corgi' comes from two Welsh words: 'cor' (small) and 'ci' (dog). Corgis were used to round up cattle at milking time.
- ★ Perhaps corgis were bred with short legs to avoid being kicked by the cows.

Pembroke Welsh Corgis
- ★ This is the more common variety.
- ★ It is believed that Pembroke corgis came to Wales with the Vikings or the Flemings (settlers from Flanders in Belgium) in the 10th or 11th century.
- ★ Queen Elizabeth II is famous for her corgis. She had her first corgi, Susan, when she was 18.

Cardigan Welsh Corgis
- ★ The Cardigan corgi has an alternative name – 'the Yard Dog' – because it measures a yard (about a metre) in length.
- ★ These days there aren't many Cardigan corgis left, but a society has been formed for their protection.

Did you know ...

Clever Dogs

★ In 2011 a Labrador from Torfaen got into the *Guinness World Records* for recycling 26,000 plastic bottles over a period of six years.

★ Tubby likes finding bottles better than chasing after his ball. He crushes them and removes the plastic top too!

Q&A

Question: How many dogs survived when the *Titanic* sank in 1912?
Answer: Three.

★ Two dogs were running after rabbits in Southerndown, near Bridgend, in 2011 when they fell 150 feet down the cliffs. The dogs received only slight injuries and suffered no long-term harm.

Old Dogs

★ A dog's **lifespan** is between 12 and 14 years, but a dog living on the Gower Peninsula reached the ripe old age of 22.

Fact!

Some foods are **toxic** for dogs, for example chocolate and onions.

Vocabulary

lifespan: the average length of time lived by an animal or a human
toxic: something poisonous which might harm or even kill you

Cats
Did you know ...

Fact!
The Romans are believed to have brought the first domestic cats to Wales. It's thought that these cats were black in colour.

Cats' claws
* In order to walk, and when they are at rest, cats retract their claws.
* Cats extend their claws when they are climbing, fighting or killing their prey.

Climbing, falling and jumping
* All cats are good climbers.
* If a cat falls, it can turn in the air so that it lands on its feet.

Q&A
Question: How high can a cat jump?
Answer: Up to seven times its own height!

Cats in the dark
* The whiskers on either side of a cat's face help it to find its way in the dark. 
* The middle of the cat's eye – the pupil – grows bigger in the dark. With more light going into the eye, it's easier for the cat to see.
* In low-light conditions, cats' eyes are six or seven times more sensitive than ours.

Vocabulary
retract: to draw back or pull something in
extend: to push something outwards or forwards
prey: a creature hunted by another for food or sport

18

Did you know ...

Fact!
A frightened cat can run at a speed of up to 31 miles an hour for a short distance.

- ★ Cats sleep for between 13 and 14 hours a day.
- ★ Cats lick themselves to keep clean.
- ★ Unlike people, cats don't sweat.

Q&A
Question: How many sets of whiskers does a cat have?
Answer: Four sets on either side of its nose.

The oldest cat in the world?
- ★ Cats have a lifespan of around 15 years, but a cat in Llanelli had its 39th birthday in 2011. Perhaps it was the oldest cat in the world!

Big Cats
- ★ Domestic cats are related to lions, tigers, jaguars, panthers, leopards, pumas and cheetahs.
- ★ A number of big cats are said to be on the loose in Wales.

tiger

lion

Land Mammals
Goats

Did you know ...

Q&A

Question: For how long have goats been bred in Wales?
Answer: For more than 1,000 years.

★ Goats give us milk, cheese, meat, and wool – mohair and kashmir.

★ Goats' milk is very good for babies and people who are ill. It's easier to digest than cows' milk.

★ Goats' eyes have rectangular-shaped pupils. They have excellent sight and can graze at night.

★ A goat's skin is soft and is used to make gloves and bags.

★ Goats live for between 10 and 12 years.

★ A white goat is the mascot of the Royal Welsh Regiment.

Fact!

A goat can catch a cold!

Vocabulary

digest: turn food in the stomach into a form the body can use
graze: nibble grass or hay

Did you know ...

★ Goats:

- are excellent swimmers
- are great jumpers
- are happy to eat all kinds of things, even clothes from the line
- are able to live on poor-quality land. One name for the goat is 'the poor man's cow'

Wild Goats

★ Wild goats live on steep cliffs and they can be seen in a number of places in Wales:

- on the mountains in Snowdonia
- on the Great Orme, above Llandudno
- on Yr Eifl, a mountain on the Llŷn Peninsula
- on Cadair Idris

★ Wild goats often cause a nuisance because they eat **crops** grown by farmers and gardeners, and scarce plants like the Snowdon Lily.

Vocabulary

crops: plants grown for food, such as vegetables and wheat

Deer
Did you know ...

Q&A

Question: How many kinds of deer are there in Britain?

Answer: Seven. You need to look at the tail to tell the difference.

★ The red deer is the largest wild animal in Wales.

★ Deer are fully grown when they measure 120 centimetres at shoulder height and when they weigh about 136 kilograms.

★ Their antlers can grow to more than 90 centimetres!

★ Fallow deer came to Wales with the Normans. Deer are quite tame in parkland settings like Margam (near Port Talbot) and Dinefwr (Llandeilo) but in the wild they are shy creatures.

★ Deer are excellent swimmers!

Rabbits
Did you know ...

★ The Normans brought rabbits to Wales in the 11th and 12th centuries.

★ People kept rabbits as a source of food.
★ Some of the rabbits escaped and were eaten by stoats and foxes.
★ In the 19th century, rabbits became a pest because there were fewer stoats and foxes.
★ In the Second World War, city people got used to eating rabbit meat.
★ Between 1953 and 1955, 98% of the Welsh rabbit population was destroyed by a disease called myxomatosis.

stoat

★ A rabbit's teeth never stop growing!
★ Rabbit poo is great for the garden.
★ Rabbits jump and spin in the air when they're happy.

Getting rid of rabbits
★ Rabbits were making holes in a rugby ground in Corwen. But after someone decided to put human hair on the pitch, the rabbits disappeared for good!

Q&A
Question: How many rabbits are kept as pets in Britain?
Answer: More than 1,000,000 (million).

Vocabulary
stoats: small furry mammals, similar to weasels and ferrets

Badgers
Did you know ...

- The old-fashioned name for the badger is Brock, which is thought to come from the Welsh word *broch* or its Scottish equivalent.
- The badger is a large animal.
- It measures almost a metre in length.
- It weighs approximately 11 kilograms.

Q&A

Question: How can you work out a badger's age?
Answer: By looking at its teeth.

The badger's home

- The badger digs an underground den or **sett** with a number of rooms. It keeps one of these as a toilet area.
- It uses the long claws on its back feet to dig the sett.
- It's probable that some badger setts are hundreds of years old. 
- The badger sleeps by day and comes out to hunt at night.
- They say that a badger's claws can dig a hole faster than a person using a spade.

Fact!

After eating rotten fruit badgers are said to behave as if they are drunk!

Vocabulary

sett: the special name for a badger's underground home

24

Did you know ...

Tasty food

★ Badgers eat:
- mice
- nuts
- toads
- snails
- snakes
- rabbits
- berries

★ They also eat up to 200 worms every day!

★ Usually three or four babies are born in the springtime.

★ A badger's sense of smell is 800 times better than that of a human.

★ A badger's fur looks grey on its back and sides but there are black and white parts to every hair.

★ Sometimes badger fur is used to make shaving brushes and hairbrushes.

★ Years ago badgers were hunted and eaten.

★ Today they get the blame for spreading TB to cattle. In 2012 the Welsh government decided to vaccinate badgers against the disease.

★ This was instead of holding a badger cull.

Vocabulary

cull: killing animals to stop disease from spreading

Squirrels
Did you know...

★ Two sorts of squirrel live in Wales – the red squirrel and the grey squirrel.

★ The red squirrel was here first.

★ The grey squirrel came from America in the 19th century and it has taken over the red squirrel's territory.

★ There are only 140,000 red squirrels left in Britain but there are 2,500,000 (2.5 million) grey squirrels.

★ The red squirrel measures 40 centimetres from nose to tail. It's a bit smaller than the grey squirrel, which is 50 centimetres in length.

★ Unfortunately, the red squirrel has practically disappeared but it can still be found:
- on Anglesey
- in the Clocaenog forest in Denbighshire
- in the Tregaron area

Q&A
Question: How much does the red squirrel weigh?
Answer: Around 275-300 grams, the same as four Mars bars!

Making the Crossing from Anglesey

★ In 2009 two squirrels were seen in the Bangor area. It's likely that they crossed the Menai Strait on one of the two bridges which link Anglesey with the mainland.

Fact!
Squirrels can hang upside down!

Vocabulary
territory: an area of land settled by people or animals

26

Did you know ...

* A squirrel's bushy tail is as long as its body.

* A squirrel can fall 30 metres without injury because its long, furry tail acts like a parachute and slows it down.

* The squirrel prepares for winter by building itself a thicker drey, out of twigs and woodland material.

* It builds up a stock of food, but sometimes comes out to forage.

* Squirrels like eating nuts and acorns.

* Sometimes they store nuts in the soil but then they forget about them or fail to find them again.

Vocabulary

drey: a squirrel's home, about the size of a football, made out of twigs and leaves
forage: hunt for food

27

Foxes
Did you know ...

★ The fox:
- is slightly smaller than a medium-sized dog, to which it is closely related
- lives both in the countryside and the town
- goes out at night to hunt rabbits and mice
- is the farmer's enemy because it kills chickens and (sometimes) young lambs
- is a very cunning animal

★ In Welsh it's often known as a *llwynog* because of its bushy tail. *Llwyn* is the Welsh word for a bush.

Fact!
A fox's hearing is so sharp, it can hear a watch ticking from a distance of 40 metres.

★ Since 2002 there has been a ban on the hunting of foxes with hounds.

★ In the days when they were hunted, a crafty fox would sometimes run through a stream or a river so that the foxhounds would lose its scent.

Vocabulary
scent: signs or traces left by humans or animals

28

Hedgehogs
Did you know ...

★ You're most likely to see hedgehogs at night.

★ When they're threatened, they roll into a prickly ball.

★ They can live for between two and seven years, but lots of hedgehogs get killed on the road.

★ Hedgehogs hibernate during the winter.

★ They are nocturnal animals.

Q&A

Question: How many spikes are there on the back of a hedgehog?
Answer: Between 5,000 and 7,000.

★ Hedgehogs:
- are full of fleas
- snore when they're asleep
- are fond of dog food 
- are very noisy eaters
- are excellent climbers 

29

Mice
Did you know ...

★ There are three main species of mice living in Wales:
- field mice
- house mice
- rats

field mouse

house mouse

rat

★ Field mice, including wood mice, live in fields, woods and hedges. They are generally larger than house mice.

★ Field mice often line their nests with feathers or wool.

★ Harvest mice live only in lowland Wales.

★ They use their long tails to grip and climb up the wheat stalk.

harvest mouse

★ House mice can live in the strangest places, even in a freezer!

★ They weigh up to 25 grams.

★ Grapes, raisins, rhubarb and walnuts are all poisonous to mice.

Fact!
Eating lettuce can give a mouse diarrhoea.

Did you know ...

★ Both black and brown rats live in Wales. The brown rat is more common.

★ Black rats came to Wales in the 12th and 13th centuries. They were responsible for spreading the Black Death, or plague.

★ One female rat can have eight litters of up to 20 young in a single year – that's 160 new rats every year!

★ An infestation of rats can do a lot of damage to crops and foodstuffs. Traps and poison are used to try to control them.

★ They say that you are never further than six metres from a rat! But it's likely to depend on where you are!

★ Rats and mice can:
  • live for a long time without water – longer than camels
  • push their way through the smallest of holes
  • gnaw through glass, wire, aluminium and lead

★ Their teeth are extremely strong!

Vocabulary

litter, litters: the number of young born at the same time to the same mother

Bats
Did you know ...

Q&A
Question: How do bats keep themselves clean?
Answer: They lick and scratch themselves for hours on end. They even wash behind their ears!

- ★ The bat is the only mammal which can fly.
- ★ Bats use echolocation to look for food and find their way around.
- ★ They make high-pitched sounds which create an echo when the sound waves come up against walls, trees or insects. This tells the bats how close they are.
- ★ There are over 1,100 bat species across the world, but only 18 species live in Britain.
- ★ Bats are nocturnal.

In your roof
- ★ Bats hang out together in hidden places. When they are at rest, they hang upside down
- ★ Sometimes thousands of bats live together.
- ★ Bats are protected by law. You are not allowed to get rid of bats if they decide to come and live in your roof.
- ★ The smallest Welsh bat, and the most common, is the Lesser Bat.
- ★ Some scarce varieties of bat live in Wales, such as the Greater Horseshoe Bat.

Lesser Bat

Greater Horseshoe Bat

Fact!
Bats always turn left when leaving a cave!